STRANGE
AFFAIRS

STRANGE
AFFAIRS

Bruce Thomas

Rough Notes Press

Bruce Thomas is the former bass player with Elvis Costello and the Attractions — which he has written about
in *Rough Notes* and *The Open Road*.

He is also Bruce Lee's principal biographer, with the best-seller *Fighting Spirit* — along with *Complete Teachings* and *A Life Worth Remembering*.

His biography of heavyweight champion Tyson Fury was a #1 Amazon best-seller.

Author's Note

Secret Affairs collates material from the deepest recesses of the internet and other sources in the public domain, to combine with my own personal experiences and encounters, to present a compendium of flawed figures from the worlds of music, media, monarchy, and more.

Beneath their carefully-managed public image and other fictional scenery, not everyone in life is who they seem. ...Just as, beneath the armour, behind the curtain, or without the disguise, neither Darth Vader, the Wizard of Oz, or Mrs Doubtfire were who they first appeared to be.

In *Strange Affairs*, I reveal a few of those I've actually brushed up against — along with a few others I'm glad I haven't. Here are innocent surprises and unexpected couples, shenanigans and betrayals, along with the darker deeds of misfits, murderers, and madmen. You may be familiar with one of two of them already, but you won't have heard it all.

Contents

John Lennon and Alma Cogan

WHEN JOHN LENNON'S first wife, Cynthia, died on the 1st of April, 2015, a few days later, a newspaper finally broke a story she'd once told a reporter back in 1989 — that it wasn't Yoko Ono who'd split the Lennon marriage, but the singer Alma Cogan.

In the 1950s, Alma Cogan was Britain's first female pop star and highest-paid entertainer. Born in 1932, she was eight years older than John Lennon. But in terms of their respective careers, those eight years were an entire generation. With her full-skirted frocks and backcombed beehive hair, in the 1960s she was seriously unhip. Even so, she was still a great one for having parties at her London home where she entertained film stars, TV personalities, and musicians — including the Beatles.

In her heyday, Alma's brio and talent brought her extraordinary fame. In a brief but meteoric career, she packed theatres all over the country and dazzled millions of TV viewers with her exuberance. Like Liberace, her style was kitsch and camp. She belted out one novelty hit after another — *Bell Bottom Blues, Dreamboat, I Can't Tell a Waltz from A Tango, Twenty Tiny Fingers, Never Do a Tango with an Eskimo, Cowboy Jimmy Joe,* and *Just Couldn't Resist Her with Her Pocket Transistor,* clocking up over twenty hits and spending an amazing 109 weeks on the charts.

When Alma was still unmarried and into her 30s, rumours swirled about her sexuality, with whispers that she was a lesbian. Two of the men who regularly escorted her, the composer Lionel Bart and Beatles manager Brian Epstein, were both gay. While one of her closest friends, the broadcaster David Jacobs, said, 'I always thought of her as a virgin.'

Sandra Caron

Alma's younger sister, Sandra Caron, a West End stage star, had got to know the Beatles before Alma, and had become 'very close' to Paul McCartney. When she later told her own story for the first time, she revealed that Alma and John Lennon had been secret lovers. 'I knew about Alma and John, of course, but it was something no-one admitted because John was married. We had a very strict Jewish upbringing and my mother would never have approved of a relationship between Alma and a married man.'

John Lennon and Alma Cogan appeared on the same bill on *Ready Steady Go*. The chemistry is there to see.

Ironically, when John and Cynthia Lennon attended art college in Liverpool, he would joke about Alma Cogan and do mocking impersonations. But in 1962, when The Beatles first appeared with her on *Sunday Night at the London Palladium,* Lennon rapidly revised his view. 'It was obvious that John was potty about her,' said George Harrison. Soon afterwards, the Fabs started visiting Alma's home in Stafford Court, on Kensington High Street, where she lived with her sister, Sandra, and her widowed mother. John called Alma 'Sara Sequin', while her mother, Fay, became 'Ma McCogie.'

Alma's home was one of the most celebrated showbiz salons in London. Princess Margaret, Audrey Hepburn, Cary Grant, Noel Coward, Ethel Merman, Danny Kaye, Sammy Davis Jr, Michael Caine, Bruce Forsyth, and Roger Moore were all visitors.

Cynthia Lennon recalls their first visit: 'John and I thought of her as out-of-date and unhip, in her old-fashioned cinched-in waists and wide skirts. But in the flesh, she was beautiful, intelligent, and funny, oozing sex appeal and charm. Walking into her home for the first time was like walking into another world. It was decorated like a swish nightclub with rich, dark silk and brocade everywhere. There were ethnic sculptures, ornaments, and dozens of photos in elaborate silver, gold, and jewelled frames.'

Cynthia Lennon 'knew' that Alma and John had become lovers. 'I could feel the sexual tension between them, and see how outrageously she flirted with him. I had no real evidence, just a strong gut feeling.' Her suspicions were correct. Alma and John, heavily disguised, took to meeting for passionate interludes in West End hotels, where they usually registered as 'Mr and Mrs Winston' (John's middle name).

On another of the Beatles' regular visits to Alma's home, it was at her piano, with Sandra at his side, that Paul McCartney composed the tune that eventually became perhaps his most-famous song *Yesterday*. It was three in the morning, and McCartney first called the tune 'Scrambled Eggs', because that's what 'Ma McCogie' had just cooked for them.

Along with emergence of the Beatles had come the rise of younger female singing stars like Lulu, Sandie Shaw, and Dusty Springfield. But even as Alma Cogan's star dimmed in Britain, in Japan her record *Just Couldn't Resist Her with Her Pocket Transistor* topped the charts for an unbelievable ten months.

John Lennon was anxious for Alma to recover a foothold in the UK charts, and tried to update her image by having her record covers of his songs, *Eight Days a Week* and *Help!* But by 1965, record producers were becoming dissatisfied with her work, and it was clear that her health was failing. One of her close friends attributed this decline to some highly-experimental and questionable injections Alma was taking to lose weight. She certainly lost the weight, but after the injections, she was never herself again. Shortly afterwards, ovarian cancer was diagnosed.

Late one October night, in 1966, in a private room in London's Middlesex Hospital, Alma lay in a coma as her young life ebbed away. Her face, once so vibrant now appeared almost skeletal. The following day, headlines informed an incredulous public that Alma Cogan had died from cancer at the age of 34. Shocked radio listeners switched on to hear her disembodied voice singing the Irving Berlin song that begins *'Heaven, I'm in heaven.'* Sandra Caron, who was now enjoying success herself, as a performer in the United States, cancelled her appearance on the Merv Griffin Show to fly back to London.

It didn't seem possible that the bouncy, bright, bubbling Alma, with her voluminous sequinned dresses, her brunette beehive, sparkling eyes, and wide smile, could be snuffed out of existence with such shocking suddenness at such a young age.

Just two weeks later, and in a highly vulnerable state, John got together with the *avant-garde* Japanese artist, Yoko Ono, who until that time had been more of an irritating fan. Yoko Ono was also older than John — much the same age as Alma had been — and soon became the woman who was to accompany (some might say dominate) the rest of his life, until he too came to a shocking and untimely end.

Maybe both Alma Cogan and John Lennon's premature deaths were so sad, because they were such a denial of what both Alma's playfulness and John's optimism presented. In the end this has to be their shared legacy. They both gave people reasons to smile.

Sly and Doris

AS A CALIFORNIA-BASED staff producer for Columbia Records, Terry Melcher was young, hip, and well-connected — a friend of the Beach Boys, and a colleague of the Byrds. He was also the son of the 1950's star Doris Day by her second husband, the musician Al Jorden — though he took the surname of his mother's third husband, Martin Melcher.

Terry Melcher made early inroads into the music industry as singer Terry Day. But when he failed to make waves, he shifted behind the mixing desk instead, and turned his attentions to production, with better results, turning out a string of middle-of-the-road hits for the likes of Pat Boone and Wayne Newton. But it was his work on eight best-selling albums for Paul Revere & The Raiders, followed by five for The Byrds, that established him as a producer of note.

Sly Stone (born Sylvester Stewart) is an American musician, most famous as the frontman of his band, Sly and the Family Stone — a band that played a crucial role in the development of soul, funk, rock, and psychedelia in the 1960s and 70s. Sly Stone was rock royalty, a superfly, a funky mother...... His friends were stars like Richard Prior and Redd Foxx.

Sly Stone and Terry Melcher met through Sly's manager. It quickly became obvious that, besides music, they shared a passion for cars. Sly had a collection of seventeen, including a yellow-and-black 1936 Cord, a Lamborghini (later confiscated by the IRS) and a 36-foot Winnebago motorhome — though whenever he did any serious travelling, it was by chauffeured stretch limo. Sly Stone and Terry Melcher also shared a passion for hedonism. Melcher lived in an enormous rented mansion with immaculately-manicured lawns on Cielo Drive in Beverly Hills. It was here that he hosted parties for the A-list of the LA hip. And it was here, when his mother Doris happened to be staying over, that she found herself in the music room with Sly Stone.

Born Doris von Kappelhoff, in Cincinnati, in 1924, she'd been a child star since the age of twelve, starting out as a dancer, until a car crash forced her to switch to singing. She became a radio and dance band singer during the 40s, quickly learning to fend off the advances of older musicians while touring, leading to her clean-cut image as 'America's last virgin.'

Her film debut came in 1948, from where she went on to star in a series of chirpy movie-musicals which played on her freckle-faced, girl-next-door cuteness. Later, more-potent on-screen chemistry followed in romantic comedies with Rock Hudson. But by 1973, she'd quit movies, even turning down the role of Mrs Robinson in *The Graduate* claiming, 'I never retired, I just did something else.'

But her life wasn't always as sunny as her personality suggested. Her 17-year marriage to Martin Melcher, who was also her manager and agent, ended bitterly. He'd always over-controlled her both as an actor and a wife, and when he died in 1968, she discovered he'd also embezzled some $22 million from her.

When Doris, in her stretch slacks and loose blouse, came sweeping down the staircase of her son's Hollywood mansion, and into the music lounge, there at the piano sat Sly Stone. On the keyboard he began picking out her famous hit tune *'Que Sera, Sera.'* (What will be, will be.) Turning on the charm, told her how much he loved her recording of that song. Showing off, and playing up his image, Sly told her, 'Si'-down girl.' She did, singing and humming along as he played, just as she'd once done in a piano-stool duet with Frank Sinatra in *Young at Heart*.

Doris was a natural comedienne and famously unflashy, but she knew how to act up too, when appropriate. Her own conversation now played on her ditzy-blonde screen persona, with affected tongue-in-cheek 'darn it', or 'for gosh sake'. Movie star and funk mother...... were mutually charmed.

Word soon leaked into the Hollywood community, about the encounter, especially when it emerged that Sly was recording his own version of her most-famous song. Doris was already known to have dated two black men, the basketball player, Elgin Baylor, and the baseball player, Maury Wills — who said Doris had the best body he'd ever seen on a woman. Her own father had married a black woman named Luvenia Williams.

But this was also the time when Captain Kirk's interracial kiss with Uhuru on the bridge of the Starship Enterprise sent shockwaves through the TV networks. Could such an unlikely liaison have been consummated? They both refused either to confirm or deny what, and if, developments had occurred. So, did they, or didn't they?

...Qué Pasó, Pasó. (What happened, happened.)

Lembit and Gabriela

FROM THE START they were dubbed the 'odd couple', though both insisted publicly that their surprise love affair was, in his words, a 'meeting of minds' and, in hers, 'like a mushroom - it could only get bigger.' The Liberal Democrat MP, Lembit Opik, and Gabriela

Irimia — one half of the hot-pant-wearing novelty pop act, the Cheeky Girls — shrugged off criticism that the relationship was a PR stunt.

In April 2008, *Hello!* Magazine revealed how Lembit had proposed with a Tiffany diamond ring, beside the Trevi Fountain in Rome. The engaged couple couldn't have chosen a showier way to prove wrong all the doubters who said it would never last.

The couple spoke of their love for each other, with Lembit glowing in his praise for his Transylvanian fiancée as his intellectual equal, despite her being 18 years his junior. Lembit described how they played Scrabble and enjoyed philosophical conversations. 'For instance, one evening we discussed the concept of a perfect circle, as a geometric challenge.'

But just three months after their Roman romance, their relationship appeared to be as dead as the use of Latin on Twitter. There was no contact for two weeks — they weren't talking at all, let alone about geometric challenges. The young singer, who'd once dedicated a song to Lembit, *Text Me, I Love You,* was now ignoring his own increasingly frantic texts as their relationship of almost two years faltered.

Gabriela's mother and manager, Margit, began sounding off about Lembit's suitability as a future son-in-law, claiming that Gabriela was on the verge of a nervous breakdown, due to rushing into the engagement while she was still grieving for her grandmother, who'd died two weeks previously.

Margit revealed how Lembit had upset 'the family' by ignoring Romanian tradition in failing to inform them of his intention to propose to her daughter. 'In Romania, a man asks the father for permission for his daughter to marry him,' huffed Margit. 'That is the tradition, but Lembit shows no understanding of our culture at all' — despite a *GQ* magazine interview where Lembit said how much he enjoyed learning about Romanian culture. 'When Gabriela came back from Rome, she said, "I know I've done wrong." But she loves Lembit and wanted to make the most of the moment. She hadn't been expecting it at all and hadn't wanted it to come that way, out of the blue.'

Lembit's former fiancée, the ITV weathergirl, Sian Lloyd, must've been rubbing her hands with glee. During their four-year relationship, she too appeared with Lembit in a glossy magazine, revealing how he'd proposed to her while he took her up in a light aircraft. She broke off their engagement shortly before his relationship with Gabriela started, tired of his partying, going off radar, and having to check newspaper columns to find out where he'd been. Sian who soon after married the motor-racing entre- preneur, Jonathan Ashman, described her break from 'oddball' Lembit as a lucky escape, and telling the Cheeky Girl she was welcome to him.

Sian Lloyd

Meanwhile, the 43-year-old Shadow Secretary for Housing was refusing to comment on reports that Gabriela had dumped him following a series of rows which came to a head at a gala dinner in London where, with her twin sister Monica, she was about to perform their hit *The Cheeky Song (Touch My Bum)*. On the evening in question, Lembit had been going on and on, as he usually did, dominating the conversation while Gabriela wanted to get ready to perform. She decided she'd had enough, stormed off and did the gig, and refused to speak further to Lembit, or leave with him. She later refused to comment.

Of course, one person who *was* prepared to comment was mother Margit, who told newspapers that, while Gabriela had refused to speak to Lembit for two weeks, she hadn't completely dumped him and was only 'taking a break.' But compared with the effusive manner in which she'd first greeted her daughter's romance with Lembit, Margit's tone had cooled considerably.

She'd even marked the date that Gabriela had first consummated her relationship with Lembit on a wall calendar in the family home. At the time, she described the pair as 'soulmates' and said of their relationship: 'It's so genuine. Gabriela believes the sparkle will stay.' But now, it seemed that the only thing with any sparkle was the engagement ring.

Any suggestion that Margit might have been exploiting Gabriela's romance to further the girls' careers was met with anger. It was Lembit, she insisted, who had benefited from his relationship with Gabriela, not the other way around. 'Lembit is famous because of Gabriela,' said Margit, forgetting that he was quite well-known when he was engaged to Sian Lloyd. 'There are hundreds of MPs, but people can remember the names of only two or three from the Liberal Democrats, which is a marginal party.' Lembit Opik finally split from his Cheeky Girl fiancée, as her mother launched one final blistering tirade, again claiming he was only ever in it for the fame. But his complicated love life was to continue.

In 2020, his pregnant fiancée, Sabina Vankova [surely not pronounced 'wank over'!] moved out of their four-bedroom house in Epsom, Surrey, and fled to Bulgaria with their four-year-old daughter, after dumping him over his 'friendship' with a female Russian colleague, Natalia Khomutinnkova, with whom he would go on 'business trips' to Paris and Nice.

But a week after fleeing, Miss Vankova, 35, discovered that she was again pregnant by the 55-year-old former politician. It wasn't the first time that Miss Vankova had walked out on him. Three years previously, she'd decamped to Bulgaria after photographs emerged of Opik with Alex Best, widow of footballer George Best, but they were later reconciled.

Opik also dated the former shop assistant, now model and part-time porn star, Katie Green, who worked on photoshoots for Wonderbra's 'larger cup sizes' — until she parted company with the lingerie firm after being asked to lose a couple of stones. In the end, though, one is forced to wonder what hidden attraction lurks behind Lembit's lopsided visage.

David Gilmour and Roger Waters

IN 1974, I'd just been sacked from my role as bass player of Sutherland Bothers and Quiver [hereafter referred to as SB&Q for obvious reasons]. During a row with Iain Sutherland (now sadly, 'the late' Iain Sutherland) about our record producer Muff Winwood, apparently, I'd gone too far. My dismissal provoked a round of musical chairs as SB&Q began casting round for a replacement for me. They homed in on Tex Comer, the bassist with Ace, a soft-rock group of the parish.

Tex Comer is the one 'floating' top left

After a brief flirtation, Tex decided to stay with Ace. So, the other Sutherland brother, Gavin, took over SB&Q bass duties. In the meantime, Ace's keyboard player, Paul Carrack, had learned of Tex's possible defection and wrote a song *How Long* about it, firmly directed at Tex.

> How long has this been going on?
> How long has this been going on?
> Oh, your friends with their fancy persuasion
> Don't admit that it's part of a scheme
> But I can't help but have my suspicions
> 'Cos I ain't quite as dumb as I seem
> And you said you was never intending
> To break up our scene this way
> But there ain't any use in pretending
> It could happen to us any day…

Most people assumed these lyrics were addressed to a wayward lover. But no, they were all about the possibility of Tex leaving Ace. *How Long* went on to enjoy 'significant chart success' in many countries, and became something of a classic — which Paul Carrack has continued to feature throughout his career, both as a solo artist, and as a member of bands like Squeeze and Eric Clapton's outfit. I am amused to think that — in a roundabout way — my getting sacked from SB&Q triggered the chain of events for this perennial hit.

Shortly after I'd been relieved of my bass-playing duties with SB&Q, I went to see them play at the Rainbow in Finsbury Park — we hadn't fallen out to the extent that I was no longer welcome at gigs. One of the other guests, loitering alongside at the venue, was Pink Floyd's David Gilmour, who was there as a friend of SB&Q's guitarist, Tim Renwick.

They both hailed from Cambridge, and the earlier incarnation of Quiver (pre-Sutherland) had shared the same manager as Pink Floyd. Gilmour was a fan of Tim's guitar playing and so had recommended us. As a result, Quiver went on to support Pink Floyd at literally dozens of gigs, over the years, and we knew each other well at this point. I was even recruited to the Pink Floyd's football team for pop group league weekend fixtures.

At the time, it was becoming obvious that Roger Waters and David Gilmour were also going to part ways at some point — maybe sooner, rather than later. At the Rainbow, David Gilmour asked if I might be interested in taking on bass playing duties with Pink Floyd. He wanted to recruit me, he said, in order to free Roger to act as a kind of MC — a narrator banging a gong and haranguing the audience through a loud hailer. ...But, thinking about it now, maybe he had longer-term plans in mind.

We'll never know what might've happened had I joined the band as I simply thought that Gilmour was joking and didn't take his remark seriously enough. As a result, I never became a member of Pink Floyd and so — unlike my potential rhythm section partner

— Nick Mason, I missed out on becoming the proud owner of a fleet of rare Ferraris.

I console myself in the certain knowledge that — just as happened with both previous and later band leaders — I would've probably ended up antagonising someone in Pink Floyd, too, and would barely have lasted long enough to make the down payment on a VW. Later events that were to come to light suggest that the fortune I thought I'd missed out on might not have been forthcoming, anyway.

Let me explain... David Gilmour joined Pink Floyd in 1968, as Syd Barrett's replacement. Roger Waters was always hesitant about the idea of collaboration with the new man, preferring to be captain of the ship. Despite the astronomical success which saw their eventual *Dark Side of the Moon* album stay on the charts for 741 weeks, with sales of 45 million, Roger Waters and David Gilmour always had something of a dysfunctional partnership. When Waters went on to leave the band in 1985, he immediately locked horns with Gilmour in a bitter legal battle that would last years, as he issued statements to EMI and CBS invoking the 'leaving member' clause in his contract.

As the main creative force in the band, Roger Waters didn't believe Pink Floyd could continue in his absence and so, in October 1986, he started High Court proceedings to formally dissolve Pink Floyd, while labelling the group as 'a spent force, creatively.' David Gilmour opposed this, stating that Pink Floyd was not going away, and that Waters couldn't declare it dead while the group was still making music. Waters eventually withdrew, saying: 'If I hadn't, the financial repercussions would have wiped me out completely.' And despite a potentially-reunited Floyd being offered $150 million for a new US tour, not even that kind of money could get Waters and Gilmour back on the road together again.

The feud between the two was put into context in a later interview with drummer Nick Mason in *Rolling Stone:*

> It's a really odd thing, in my opinion, but I think the problem is that Roger doesn't really respect David. He feels that writing is everything and that guitar playing and the singing are something that, I won't say anyone can do, but that everything should be judged on the writing rather than the playing. I think it rankles with Roger that he made a sort of error in a way that he left the band assuming that without him it would fold.

Gilmour didn't hold back when he eventually gave his own opinions on his former bandmate to the same magazine:

> Why on Earth anyone thinks what we do now would have anything to do with him is a mystery to me. Roger was tired of being in a pop group. He is very used to being the sole power behind his career. The thought

of him coming into something that has any form of democracy to it, he just wouldn't be good at that. Besides, it's over half a lifetime away. We really don't have that much in common anymore.

If anything, the animosity has increased rather than diminished over the years. When Roger Waters made one final attempt at a peace summit, at an airport hotel, it ended in disaster, and confirmed that there would never be a truce between the two.

In the end, Roger Waters hired the great Snowy White as his guitarist; while Gilmour's Floyd recruited former Quiver guitarist, Tim Renwick, and replaced Roger Waters with the session bassist Guy

Pratt, after using the flavour-of-the-month session man, Pino Palladino for a time. Guy Pratt went on to marry Floyd keyboardist Rick Wright's daughter, Gaia, and opened his groom's speech with: 'I'm only hear today because Pino couldn't make it.'

But more to the point, it turned out that both Guy Pratt and Tim Renwick were only ever paid wages, hired as session men, rather than enjoying part of a band split. And that would undoubtedly have been my fate, had I ever joined the band. And so, I would have never been caught speeding down Chiswick High Road in an F40.

Even Rick Wright himself had suffered this fate... Delays to the recording sessions for *The Wall* album caused it to overrun. Wright had a holiday booked and wasn't prepared to cancel it, and was fired as a result. When he later 're-joined' the band to tour and promote the album, he was hired as a salaried musician only, on wages. But ironically, as the staging for the tour was so elaborate and expensive, he was actually the only one who made any money out of it.

Just as I did myself, Guy Pratt went on to have his own signature bass produced in collaboration with Barry Moorhouse's Bass Centre. Where mine is the P-Bass style Profile model, in a fetching shade of Salmon Pink, Guy has a J-style bass in an attractive Burgundy Mist.

When asked if he was about to go out on the new round of gigging that David Gilmour was planning to undertake, he replied that Gilmour was getting even more unbearable to be with as, year on year, his gripes about Roger Waters had turned from continual carping into an all-consuming obsession.

The decades-long feud between Roger Waters and David Gilmour, took an even deeper personal turn on in February 2023 when the latter's wife, the feminist writer, Polly Samson, who had now become one of the band's primary lyricists, took a very public swing at Waters.

> Sadly @rogerwaters you are antisemitic to your rotten core. Also, a Putin apologist and a lying, thieving, hypocritical, tax-avoiding, lip-syncing, misogynistic, sick-

with-envy, megalomaniac. Enough of your nonsense.

Gilmour 'liked' the tweet, as users on the platform quickly noted. He later made his support more obvious, tweeting: 'Every word demonstrably true.' Hours later, Waters' camp posted to Instagram:

> Roger Waters is aware of the incendiary and wildly-inaccurate comments made about him on Twitter by Polly Samson, which he refutes entirely. He is currently taking advice as to his position.

Samson's broadside seems to have been in response to a recent interview in which Waters stood by previous comments in which he likened Israel's leader Netanyahu to a dictator, and saw Russian President Vladimir Putin's 'invasion' of Ukraine as actually being a clean-up operation of the bioweapons' labs and missile sites that had gradually been positioned on Russia's doorstep, with the obvious purpose of a future invasion. Waters deemed it sad that his ex-bandmate had recorded a pro-Ukraine protest song under the Pink Floyd banner.

There then followed the predictable push to have Waters cancelled. Gilmour's wife found plenty of allies among the usual suspects — like *The Guardian* and the *BBC* — who were only too happy to jump on board, as they aimed to turn Waters' parodies of a fascist dictator into expressions of admiration. If that were true, then Charlie Chaplin's parody of Hitler in his film *The Great Dictator* would open Chaplin (himself a Jew) to exactly the same charge.

It's important, here, to challenge the synthetic ignorance of those pretending not to know what *The Wall* is really about, and who are now attempting to use it for Waters' cancellation, even though he has been performing it for over 40 years.

For those more awake than 'woke,' it's Roger Waters who holds the higher ground. When Facebook/Meta's Mark Zuckerberg wanted to use *The Wall* as a theme song to help solidify the hegemony of news and social media, government, the justice system, security agencies, pharma corporations, and all the rest of it. Waters told him simply to 'fuck off.'

While Roger Waters has shown himself to be a man of some intelligence and integrity, ironically, it was Samson's son by her first marriage, Charlie, who, at a demo to protest student tuition fee increases, was photographed dangling from a Union Jack flag at the Cenotaph war memorial. The 21-year-old said he was caught up in the moment and didn't realise it was the Cenotaph. (Hmm. At the time, he was reading History at Cambridge. I hope he got a refund.)

Brian Jones

I WAS ONLY EVER PRESENT ONCE at a conversation between David Gilmour and Mick Jagger, and it was a very brief one... At the time, Quiver had been chosen to play at the party the Stones held at a riverside inn, by the Thames, at Bray. There was a small stage in a large room set out like a school dining hall with rows of tables and benches. Many of the great and good were there. On the table immediately in front of us sat Jimmy Page and John and Yoko, all looking equally disinterested in our soft-rock meanderings.

As I mentioned, Quiver shared a manager with Pink Floyd and so Mr Gilmour had come along with us for the evening. After our mercifully short set, the buffet reopened. I was hovering on the periphery of the guests, when David Gilmour appeared with a plate piled as high with Beluga caviar as if it were a takeaway curry.

Shortly after, Mick Jagger sauntered over and looked at the mountain of fish eggs and with raised eyebrows, glanced at Gilmour and asked: 'Everything alright for you?'

The Stones with manager, Andrew Oldham.

But I'd lost any real interest in the Rolling Stones, many years before, when Brian Jones went. For me, as for many others, Brian Jones was most-charismatic member of the band, with the best haircut and clothes. He was the most popular with the girls, who wanted to be his girlfriend, and with the boys too, who wanted to be as cool as him. When he left, so did I. At the time, I knew little of the goings-on behind the scene, but as events gradually came to light, my instincts were proved right.

Yes, Brian Jones was an imperfect human, but his musical legacy demands appraisal. Like many others, I've come to realize, and then despise, the marginalization of Brian's contributions by certain members of the band — the band that Brian himself founded and recruited.

In addition to not being recognized as the band's founder, Brian was never credited for helping compose some of the most iconic Rolling Stones songs. While he wasn't the exclusive writer and composer of this material, he gave the songs life far beyond what Keith Richards' and/or Mick Jagger's contributions did. And let's not forget, their first four hits were all cover versions: of Chuck Berry's *Come On*, the Beatles' *I Wanna Be Your Man*, Buddy Holly's *Not Fade Away*, and Howling Wolf's *Little Red Rooster*.

But by the time of the *Aftermath* album, Brian had got a decent enough R&B band thinking outside of the box. At the recording session, *Under My Thumb* was going nowhere until it was discovered that a Baja

Marimba band, a novelty Mexican outfit, had left their instruments — including a marimba — in a corner of the large studio. Brian went over and started improvising on it. After a few minutes he came up with what Eddie Kramer (one of the engineers) described as 'a piece of genius ...a riff that makes sense of what would've been a nonentity.' 'Without the Marimba part, it's not really a song, is it?' said bassist Bill Wyman.

Manager Andrew Oldham, said of Brian's work on *Aftermath*: 'Brian's contribution can be heard on every track of those recordings. What that guy didn't already play, he went out and learned. You can hear his colour all over songs like *Lady Jane* or *Paint It Black*. In some instances, it was more than an embellishment; sometimes Brian pulled the whole record together.'

In her autobiography, Marianne Faithfull describes the moment in the studio when Brian first plays, on a recorder, the lilting melody that would eventually become *Ruby Tuesday*. Brian tells Keith that it's a cross between John Dowland's *Air on the Late Lord Essex* and a Skip James blues. 'Brian wanted everyone to say, "That's great Brian, wonderful!" But of course, nobody did.' When it was released, Ruby Tuesday carried the standard 'Jagger-Richards' songwriting credit. But Ruby Tuesday was written by Brian Jones with collaboration from Keith Richards. Mick had nothing to do with it — with neither with the lyrics nor the melody — but he and Keith took the writing credit.' [And no doubt all the royalties.]

The troika of Jagger, Richards, and Oldham conspired more and more gradually to separate Brian Jones from his due.

Bill Wyman (like Guy Pratt and myself) also released his own signature-model instrument with the Bass Centre. Over the years, Bill Wyman has said a lot about the situation with Brian:

> Andrew undoubtedly pushed Keith against Brian for second place in the band behind Mick ...to project them as a coupling. Brian knew he was the more-competent musician, and much more original than any of us, and his confidence in that held him for a while. But they whittled away at him and he left it too long to fight back.

> I was as close to Brian as anyone around the Stones, especially when he was made the outcast. The methods used to wear him down were terrible to watch. Andrew would turn off his mike (without his knowledge) when we were recording; or fade out his instrument. It was a closed shop.

> Brian was locked into a defensive position from which he would never return. When the manager of a group has pitted two strong, ambitious guys, who shared a flat,

against a sensitive guy with the
personality complications of Brian Jones,
only one team can win.

When I did the riff for *Miss You* — which
made the song, and which every band in
the world copied for the following year —
it still said Jagger/Richards. When I wrote
the riff for *Jumping Jack Flash*, that
became Jagger/ Richards. And that's the
way it was. It just became part and parcel
of the way the band functioned.

No wonder then, that Bill Wyman is one of Brian
Jones' greatest champions, as he confirms that the
Stones always was Jones' band, and that the rest of
the group was invited into it.

When I joined, Brian was setting up our
shows, deciding which songs we played
and recorded, and signing all the
management and recording contracts.
Brian was making all the creative and
business decisions on behalf of the band
during this time.

Among Bill Wyman's other assertions is that the
true composer for *Paint it Black* was Brian, who

developed the tune while jamming with Charlie Watts, adding, 'It's really the rhythm section and the sitar riff that drives the song and captures its Middle Eastern flavour.

The fact that the song once again credits Jagger-Richards as composers adds to evidence of their takeover of the band. There was a definite agenda at work. Jagger and Richards were seeking to be a songwriting partnership to rival Lennon and McCartney, by giving the appearance that they were the chief songwriters of the band, especially for the kind of 'artistic' songs that could give the Beatles a run for their money.

The desire of Jagger and Richards to hide Brian Jones' role stemmed from the public rivalry between the Beatles and the Stones, fuelled by John Lennon's accurate taunt that, 'the Stones aren't in the same fucking class as the Beatles.' As they sought to rival Lennon and McCartney, they hogged undeserved credit though, ironically, Lennon and McCartney wrote separately most of the time. The tragic aspect of Jagger and Richards' refusal to credit Jones, was that they'd taken the theft further and stolen the entire band from him.

By 1968, was Brian Jones truly so drug-addled that he could no longer function? We're asked to accept the inferences of Jagger and Richards, who've always seemed more than comfortable with not giving credit where it's due.

And then, on July 3, 1969, Brian was found drowned in his swimming pool. Within a week of his sudden death at the age of 27. he was replaced by guitarist Mick Taylor from John Mayall's Bluesbreakers. Mick Taylor played with the Rolling Stones from 1969 to 1974, and he, too, would go on to learn how the Stones operated.

While the Stones were working on the *It's Only Rock 'n Roll* album in Munich, Taylor couldn't make it to some of the recording sessions because he had to undergo surgery for acute sinusitis. In October

1974, ahead of the album's release, Taylor told *NME* journalist, Nick Kent, that he co-wrote two songs with Mick Jagger – *Till the Next Goodbye* and *Time Waits for No-One*. But when Kent showed him the record sleeve, Taylor's name didn't appear as a writing credit, even though Jagger had promised him it would. In December, while the other Stones were partying in London, Taylor told Jagger he was leaving the band.

Mick Taylor was a serious upgrade on Keith Richards in terms of blues-rock lead guitar work. But, in losing Brian Jones, the band had lost someone who, through a musical motif here or counter melody there, could elevate a song into something special. The Stones now became a straightforward 'it's only rock and roll' band — the character and invention replaced by repetition and cliche, tried and true, and boring to many ...including me.

In business, what happened to Brian Jones would be termed 'a hostile takeover.' He was driven out of his own band by those creating a myth that he'd lost the ability to function. But this assertion doesn't stack up against his musical contributions to the last album he did with the band: *Beggar's Banquet*. The notion that he was too out-of-it to contribute any further was the excuse used — and his death the following year put an end to the sorry tale.

Before the Stones' concert in Hyde Park — just a few days after Brian's death — Jagger's tribute 'for Brian, alright' — a verse of Shelley read in his most-affected yob voice, while wearing a little white 'skirt' — was neither sincere nor heartfelt. Though it must be said that Charlie Watts was always a great drummer, the tuneless shambles that ensued only showed what was missing ...with Jagger (as John Lennon famously put it) 'wiggling his arse with all his stupid faggot dancing.'

Brian Jones died in what will always remain both controversial and suspicious circumstances. And although they've been examined, analysed, and speculated upon many, many times ...they've never been explained adequately. We've never had any ...er ...satisfaction.

E.C. & B.B.

BACK IN THE DAY, before there was internet shopping, bands that undertook their first U.S. tours would find all kinds of booty awaiting. Every touring musician would be thrilled to acquire a Maglite (a heavy metal torch you could hit burglars over the head with) — or a pair of Red Wing boots. And, of course, there was Schwarz's wonderful toy store in New York.

On one of Elvis Costello and the Attractions' early U.S. tours, we appeared at Hollywood High School (motto: 'Achieve the Honorable') as part of our manager Jake Rivera's policy of playing unusual venues. In the audience that evening was the American model, Bebe Buell: a Playboy 'Playmate of the Month', and companion to many rock luminaries who'd had liaisons with her. The short list included Steven Tyler (with whom she had a daughter, Liv), Todd Rundgren, Jimmy Page, Mick Jagger, David Bowie, Ron Wood, Rod Stewart, and Jack Nicholson. As our friend and producer Nick Lowe remarked 'she wasn't one to let the grass grow under her back.'

But Bebe denied that she was 'a groupie', saying she considered herself as more of 'a muse.' The Attractions, considered her as more 'a-muse-ing' — because it soon turned out that Bebe had recently become quite taken with our Elvis. Maybe she saw him in a kind of Marilyn vs Arthur Miller kind of way. But he wasn't one to miss the opportunity to promote our latest album *This Years Model* and get some publicity out of it.

There are very few images of the devoted couple.

Now, at this point, you need to know that, between ourselves, the Attractions referred to our illustrious vocalist as 'the Pod' — an ungenerous reference to the fact that, owing to frequent visits to the desert trolley, he'd was coming increasingly to resemble one of those alien infiltrators pictured the sci-fi classic, *Invasion of the Body Snatchers*.

Anyway, the point is that, one day, while sitting around on the tour bus, during a lull, our drummer Pete Thomas looked at EC and raised a quizzical eyebrow...

'So...' he said, with perfect comic timing '...so Bebe ...and EC? ...So, that's Rod ...Todd ...and Pod?'

Stifled sniggering ensued. But better was yet to come...

Someone had recently bought a novelty toy to take home — an educational toy that none of us had seen before, known as a 'Speak and Spell' ™.

The toy would ask you to, for example, 'spell cat'.

On the keyboard, you typed in the letters 'C-A-T,' then hit a button to check the result.

The machine would repeat the original word, play back your answer, and then tell you if it was right or wrong.

'Cat — C-A-T — that is correct'.

But if you misspelled a word, it would also tell you.

'Cat — D-O-G — that is wrong.'

It also read numbers and did simple sums.

'2 plus 2 equals 4, that is correct.'

So now all we had to do when it asked you to spell 'dog' was to enter: E-C-I-C-U-R-4-B-B.

When EC came into the middle lounge, the Speak and Spell was lying innocently on the table. Quietly, someone reached a finger forward and pressed the 'check answer' button.

Out of the blue came this mechanical voice...

'Dog. EC — I see you are for Bebe — that is wrong!'

'What the fuck's that!' he said.

As it turned out, our EC was only to be a stepping stone from old-skool figures like Rod Stewart and Todd Rundgren to more-current ones, like the Dead Boys, Stiv Bators – though images of the couple often mistake the two and caption him as 'Costello.'

...One can't help wondering if, as a schoolboy, the young Master Bators endured an awful lot of teasing.

Margaret and Bindon

I NEVER MET PRINCESS MARGARET, but I discovered where she was, and what she was doing. Let me explain...

Three doors down from the cottage where I now live in Wiltshire is the one where Princess Margaret used to enjoy her secret weekend trysts with the landscape gardener, Roddy Llewellyn, that went on for over seven years — from 1973 until 1980. As the 'spare' to Queen Elizabeth, as other spares are prone to do, she got into some ill-advised liaisons. Perhaps the most ill-advised of these was with John Bindon — but more about that bastard in a moment...

Margaret was the better looking of two sisters and, in her younger years, was a true beauty. When she was only fourteen, she met Captain Peter Townsend, an RAF officer who had been interviewed by Margaret's father, King George VI, for the position of equerry. Their romance began eight years later, when the 22-year-old Margaret fell in love with Peter soon after the death of her father in 1952.

Said the captain: 'She was a girl of unusual, intense beauty, confined as it was in her short, slender figure and large purple-blue eyes, generous, sensitive lips, and a complexion as smooth as a peach.'

The first time the public became aware of their relationship was at Elizabeth's coronation in 1953, when the Margaret was seen to remove a piece of fluff from the captain's uniform while they were standing outside Westminster Abbey. The gesture was a sure sign that rumours of their romance were true. The news was soon printed in newspapers around the world.

But being already-divorced, Townsend's status made it impossible for Margaret to marry him, and both the Church of England and Parliament came out firmly against the match. At that time, divorcees weren't allowed to remarry in the Church of England, on top of which, Margaret would require her sister's permission to wed before the age of twenty-five.

Torn between loyalty and love for her sister, but also having to appease Parliament and the Church, Queen Elizabeth asked Margaret to pause her plans and defer making any final decisions. Eventually, after massive public support for the union, it was agreed that the two could marry, but the consequences would be steep. Margaret would have to relinquish her position, her prestige, and (more crucially) her privy purse allowance.

It was Margaret who was now caught in a clash of loyalty, forced to choose between royal duty (and income) and the man she wanted to marry She eventually decided: '...conscious of my duty to the Common-wealth, I have resolved to put these considerations before any others.'

In 1960, Margaret got engaged to the fashion photographer Anthony Armstrong-Jones, but their union was ill-fated, and they filed for divorce in 1978 — the first divorce in the royal family for 400 years. By that time, Armstrong-Jones had become disenchanted with the once-beautiful princess, saying that she looked more like 'a Jewish manicurist.'

Margaret had gained a reputation on the social circuit as someone who had to be constantly amused and entertained to the point of her hosts' exhaustion

— her visits became dreaded. She engaged in several high-profile relationships, including the romance with Roddy Llewellyn (who was 17 years younger), and the actors Peter Sellers, Warren Beatty, and Peter O'Toole.

But some of her flings were more ill-advised than others, like that with the thoroughly-nasty John Bindon, a B-list actor, who worked as an enforcer for Led Zeppelin's morbidly-obese manager, Peter Grant.

Margaret was a notorious for hedonist and would let loose completely when she was at her Caribbean holiday home on Mustique. Bindon spent three weeks there with her. His party trick — widely known in his circles — was to hang five half-pint beer tankards from his erect manhood. It's fair to assume that Margaret herself might have hung from it once or twice. Whatever the case, Bindon was certainly the biggest fucking prick I've ever encountered. Let me explain...

Back in the day, when Elvis and the Attractions were signed to Stiff Records, so were a great band called Rockpile, which featured Nick Lowe (also our record producer) and Dave Edmunds. But Dave Edmunds decided that greater things were his preferred career trajectory and declared his wish to leave the band and take up a solo career, with Peter

Grant as his manager. A showcase gig for Grant's benefit was arranged to take place in the upstairs room of a pub in Hammersmith, which we all went along to, to make up the numbers.

My wife Suzanne and I arrived in good time and bagged a table, centre stage, at the front, where we happily chatted to friends and colleagues ...until Grant and his goon Bindon arrived minutes before Dave Edmunds was due on stage. They made their way to where my wife and I were sitting. 'MOVE!' hissed Bindon, as he manhandled Suzanne from her chair and shot me a look of the kind of malice and menace, I've only ever seen that once.

You just wouldn't argue with a psychopath like that. The whole experience left a sour and bitter taste, like the feeling you get when you've been burgled or mugged, or suffered some other violence. I remained angry about it for a long time, as I watched and waited, eager to hear of any misfortune that might befall him.

John Bindon began his career as a petty criminal in London when he was still in his teens, and spent most of his time in juvenile detention centres. In his early twenties, a film director spotted him in a pub and thought him ideal for the part of a petty criminal – as all he would have to do is play himself. He got further work in films and TV, always playing the thug.

Off-screen, he was notorious for his violent temper and his habit of provoking fights in pubs for no other reason than to prove he was 'a hard man.' One evening, after such an altercation, there was blood everywhere, when he bit a man's thumb clean off. Bindon kept the thumb in a matchbox to show to people. On the *Performance* movie set, Mick Jagger was genuinely shocked to see it.

Just a year before my own encounter with Bindon, he was involved in a knife fight at a private London club. He himself was badly injured, but his opponent, a gangster called John Darke, died from the knife wounds. Bindon was tried for the murder but pleaded self-defence and was acquitted after a glowing character reference from Bob Hoskins.

But the case damaged his reputation, and coupled with being seen by directors as difficult to work with, his acting career went into decline. During the 1980s, Bindon became a recluse, spending more and more time at his Belgravia flat. He died at the age of fifty — some say from cancer, some say from AIDS.

But hey! Let's not end on a down beat and a sour note. Remember Rockpile? Rockpile once toured America with the Attractions. We travelled together on the same bus and stayed in the same hotels.

One morning. one member of Rockpile — I'm not saying who it was, apart from that he was Scottish and his name was Billy (second left) — anyway, he got up one morning and went to the door of his room to collect the newspaper he'd ordered the night before — newspapers were left outside the room in the corridor. As he reached down to pick it up, the door behind him swung shut. He stood there in the corridor, stark naked, without a key to get back in his room.

Fortunately, the newspaper in his hands was a spreadsheet and not a tabloid. He carefully unfolded it, and by means of improvised and intuitive origami, using neatly interlocking folds, he fashioned a kind of newsprint kilt that he could hold around his waist. Thus attired, he appeared shortly afterwards at the hotel front desk to explain his predicament and secure a duplicate room key. Nobody batted an eyelid.

Elizabeth and 'Porchie'

THE MARRIAGE OF QUEEN ELIZABETH II to Prince Philip, the Duke of Edinburgh, was rumoured to be fraught with affairs and infidelity. It's said that the Duke would often disguise himself as a humble delivery-van driver, in white coat and flat cap, to travel to his assignations. It's also been alleged that he was part of 'the Cliveden set' that included Dr Stephen Ward and Christine Keeler — a story that would obviously be buried by the Establishment. But there's another alleged affair that was covered-up for decades.

Throughout the 1950s and '60s, the Queen's horseracing manager, Lord Harry Porchester, and Elizabeth spent many hours together discussing racing. She spent a great deal of time with him, and they would meet frequently at the Broadlands home of Earl Mountbatten, where they would ride together, walk for hours with the dogs, and sit and talk long into the night. He was one of only a small handful of people who was allowed direct contact to the Queen.

Mountbatten was so concerned by Elizabeth's infatuation with the handsome Harry Porchester that he wrote her a warning letter, urging her to be more discreet. Elizabeth took little notice of 'Uncle Dickie's' advice and continued to see much of 'Porchie'. Though the couple would now spend fewer weekends at Broadlands, they would travel abroad on racing business, spending weekends together — even visiting Kentucky together during the spring yearling sales.

On 1 January, 1990, cabinet papers released under the 30-year rule confirmed that the Royal Family had been discussed on three occasions in 1959, but the subject matter was so sensitive for them to be kept secret for much longer than usual – locked away for 100 years, and not to be revealed until 2059. This was without precedent in peace time. What could possibly be serious enough to warrant this level of secrecy?

1959 is the year that Prince Andrew was conceived. There are many who have noted how Prince Andrew has grown to bear a resemblance to Porchester, with the similarity going beyond any facial likeness. Unlike the other children in the royal family, who are similar to Philip — tall, balding, with long faces, prominent ears, and large noses — Andrew is stocky, like Porchester, and just like the two sons born to Porchester's own marriage.

Tellingly, the Palace has never legally challenged any public statements to this effect. But the Queen's press secretary has said that suggestions of an affair were, 'very distasteful and totally unfounded. The Queen is the last person in the world to have ever considered looking at another man. Not only is this muckraking – this is gossip that's been washing around for decades. It's got absolutely no substance.'

Ohers say that the opposite is true and that Elizabeth actually wanted to have Porchester's child, as a 'love child', and how it's obvious that, despite Andrew's behaviour, which has gone completely beyond the acceptable, he always remained her clear favourite.

Of course, this isn't the first or last time that the parentage of various royals has been called into question. Aside from the much-cited likeness of Prince Harry to his mother's lover, James Hewitt, there's also the likeness of her other son, William, to King Juan Carlos of Spain. Princess Diana is rumoured to be just one of the many young women the king pursued in a romantic career in which he's said to have bedded more than five-thousand lovers.

There's a revealing photograph, taken on a 1986 holiday, that shows the Spanish king's keen interest in William, while Prince Charles looks on. On the face of things, it looks like an ordinary family snap. Juan Carlos sits with the young William, while a radiant Diana, with a protective arm round toddler Prince Harry, leans in to share a pleasantry with the good-looking monarch. At the other end of the couch, Prince Charles seems scarcely part of the same party as he stares glumly ahead like the proverbial gooseberry.

Now if any of this is true, there are implications for a grave constitutional crisis. Because if the now-King *isn't* the father oi either of his two sons, then there is no legitimate heir to the throne, and the line of succession ends.

But there's an additional frisson to all of this. An Australian man, Simon Charles Dorante-Day, claims that *he* is a secret love-child of Charles and Camila, — born in 1965, when Charles was 17 and Camilla,18, — who was then spirited away to the other side of the world. But, even if *this* is true, his illegitimacy would render him, er... illegitimate to succeed to the throne.

Charles and Savile

THE BRITISH TV PRESENTER Jimmy Savile was a serial paedophile who, during his lifetime, remained immune from capture through ostentatious charity work coupled with his befriending of the great and good. Senior members of the West Yorkshire Police were regulars at his house for tea. He spent Christmas with the Prime Minister, Margaret

Thatcher, and advised the heir to the throne Prince Charles — as well as receiving an honorary knighthood from the Pope.

For many years, Prince Charles corresponded regularly with Savile, appealing to him for help with PR. The letters show the trust that Charles put in Savile. He was trying to appeal to the British people and wanted to modernize, and saw Savile as a conduit to that. In hindsight, it was an unwise decision.

Letters between Charles and Savile shed light on the trust the prince placed in the presenter. In response to one of these requests, Savile sent Charles a handwritten guide on how to deal with the media in crisis situations. This document appears to have been passed on to Queen Elizabeth and Prince Philip. On January 27, 1989, Charles wrote to Savile:

> I attach a copy of my memo on disasters which incorporates your points and which I showed to my father. He showed it to H.M.

In another letter he asked 'Jimmy' to consult with Prince Andrew's wife, Fergie, saying:

> I wonder if you would ever be prepared
> to meet my sister-in-law, the Duchess
> of York? I can't help feeling that it
> would be extremely useful to her if you
> could. I feel she could do with some of
> your straightforward common sense.

In April 1990, Charles wrote to Savile, asking him to cast an eye over the draft of a speech he was working on. After the event, he wrote back, saying:

> I can't tell you how grateful I am for the
> most useful assistance you have
> provided for my speech in the Guildhall
> the other day. It was really good of you
> to take the trouble to put together
> those splendid notes and provide me
> with considerable food for thought.

Savile even had a hand in selecting a private secretary for Charles [the British equivalent of a chief of staff] during a period in the 1980s when Charles burned through four in seven years. He asked Savile to vet Christopher Airy, a former major-general in the British army. A bewildered Airy was interviewed in Kensington Palace by Savile, who was wearing a silver jump suit. With Savile's nod he got the job.

Charles sent Savile a box of Havana cigars — a gift he'd earlier received from Fidel Castro — with a note:

> Nobody will ever know what you've
> done for this country, Jimmy.

Weeks after his second son was born in 1984, the heir to the throne even suggested Savile as Prince Harry's godfather and included him in a draft list. The name 'James Wilson Vincent Savile, OBE' was reportedly seen on this list by Charles' private secretary, Edward Adeane.

Charles was quite correct when he stated that nobody would ever know what 'Jimmy' had done. And they didn't — not until after his death, when his many crimes came to light. But even throughout Savile's lifetime rumours abounded, as those that could've done something were forced to turn a blind eye, so complete was Savile's seduction of the establishment.

Savile wasn't publicly exposed until after his death, when around six hundred people were eventually found to have been attacked and abused by him. A subsequent inquiry found that this mainly involved children and young people, including many hospital inpatients — some as young as just two-years-old — as well as mentally-ill patients receiving treatment At one hospital, a former nurse said that he'd, 'mucked about in the morgue.'

Savile died two days before his 85th birthday, in 2011. His grave in Scarborough was positioned high on a hill, overlooking the sea — a triple headstone in black marble with gold letters that read, 'it was good while it lasted', and described him as a 'philanthropist, TV presenter, DJ, marathon runner, cyclist, wrestler, and chieftan[sic] of Lochaber Highland Games'.

But the steel coffin, gold painted, had been further encased in concrete as a 'precautionary measure.' The funeral director said, 'We felt it was better to backfill the grave with concrete to provide a secure foundation for the memorial and so that the grave couldn't and wouldn't be opened again,' saying that people might rob the grave looking for jewellery

Savile may have been buried with. But others knew full well what might happen once his crimes came to light.

Undertakers later removed the £4,000 stones in the dead of night, smashed them, and sent them to landfill, leaving Savile, encased in concrete and steel, in an unmarked grave. A campaign to have the body exhumed and cremated failed, as no one was prepared to pay to do it. Meanwhile, locals were left furious and changed their own funeral plans to avoid being laid to rest anywhere near Savile.

𝄢

During my musical career, I was to encounter Jimmy Saville several times. The first was comical; but the subsequent meetings gradually got darker and darker. When my old band Quiver did a live performance from the BBC theatre in London's Regent Street, Saville was the presenter. Throughout the day, various members of the band [OK, it was just me] took great delight in uttering his bizarre catch phrases, 'now then, now then, now then' — and doing that peculiar donkey-like braying sound he was likely do every so often.

As we were about to go on stage, we were just wating for Saville to appear and announce us, when I couldn't resist one more, 'err-uhh, err-uhh, err-uhh'.

'Shut up, you daft bastard, he'll hear you!' said one of the road crew, who was standing next to me. ...Only this time it hadn't been me, but Savile himself who, at that precise moment, stepped out from the wings to give us a withering look.

Many years later, Elvis and Attractions appeared on *Jim'll Fix It*. The idea of the show was that kids would write in with some ambition or other and Jim would 'fix it' for it to happen. Supposedly, a young boy of about ten had written in saying his greatest wish in all the world was to be our sound mixing engineer. A highly-unlikely story to start with. He probably wrote in wanting to fly a jet fighter at 100 feet along the coast, or do a few laps in an F1 car. But the BBC would've written back, mindful of the fact that record companies paid-for slots to promote their bands, and Jim's program was perfect for that. There may have been brown envelopes containing cash involved, but that is only scandalous speculation with no foundation in reality. Much.

Come the day of the show, the young lad brought his older brother along with him, but we all made sure that the boy was never left alone at any point. The rumours of Savile's peccadillos were already well known by then. We asked one of the floor cameramen, if it was true. 'Oh, that's just Jimmy,' he said, as if to confirm that they turned a blind eye to it.

But not everyone turned a blind eye to it. There were a couple of showbusiness personalities brave enough to voice their concerns about Jimmy Savile at the time. One was the magician/comedian Jerry Sadowitz who was definitely not what you would call 'a family entertainer'.

In a show at Edinburgh Assembly Rooms, in 1987, Sadowitz 'joked':

> There have been serious allegations of child abuse in Cleveland. To my mind there is only one way to find out whether this is true or not and that's to — CALL IN JIMMY SAVILE! You can't afford to fuck about! Bring in an expert! Am I right? A friend of mine reckons Jimmy Savile is a paedophile. That's why he does all the fucking charity work: it's to gain public sympathy, for when his fucking case comes up.

Sadowitz's act had been recorded for a live album, which was released, but immediately withdrawn. Yet if Sadowitz, a fringe comic with no TV or radio exposure at the time, knew enough to comment about Savile in 1987, it's fair to presume others knew, too — people who remained very quiet, when it would've needed only one or two voices to speak out.

Savile was careful in his choice of victims. He selected those who were most vulnerable, and least likely to be believed. Newspapers would have been terrified of a legal challenge from such a popular national figure.

Yet another who did speak out — at great personal cost. was John Lydon, aka Sex Pistols' singer Johnny Rotten. In an interview done as far back as 1978, Lydon said that Savile was into, 'all sorts of seediness … we all know about it but we're not allowed to talk about it.' He went on to tell the interviewer that he'd like to kill Jimmy Savile. These remarks were enough to get him banned from appearing on TV or radio for the rest of his career.

In his 2000 documentary on Savile, journalist Louis Theroux questioned him over rumours that he was sexually interested in children. In part of a chilling exchange, Savile said: 'We live in a very funny world. And it's easier for me, as a single man, to say I don't like children, because that puts a lot of salacious tabloid people off the hunt. Theroux tried to report sexual abuse carried out by Savile after a woman came forward and told him she'd been abused, along with others, when she was fifteen.

Louis Theroux recalled:

> At the time [of the 2000 documentary], I'd
> done my best to be tough with him. I
> knew he was weird and, with all his
> mannerisms, rather irritating - I had no
> interest in making a soft piece about 'the
> Charity Fundraiser'. The dark rumours of
> sexual deviance, of being unemotional, of
> having a morbid interest in corpses - were
> one of the reasons I'd taken him on as a
> subject.

All that is known, what follows is conjecture. But it's speculation that's not entirely without foundation — and it is still dangerous territory to walk in.

In 1999, on a leafy London street, the TV host Jill Dando was returning from a shopping trip and had just arrived at her front door when she was approached by a gunman who fired a single shot at point-blank range. Fifteen minutes later, she was found on her doorstep by a passer-by, but paramedics couldn't save her and the 37-year-old was declared dead at Charing Cross Hospital. A gunman had taken the life of one of the most-loved presenters on TV, to send shockwaves throughout the nation.

In July 2001, a local man, Barry George, was jailed for her murder, but the conviction was overturned seven years later, when it was judged that his IQ was too low for him to have defended himself or executed such a killing. It often happens that when there is a shocking death someone has to be caught quickly, and then when the shock has worn off, it's admitted that 'a mistake' was made, once people have moved on to other concerns.

There were several theories as to why Jill Dando had been killed. Perhaps the most convincing is that, in 2014, according a friend and BBC colleague, she'd been on the verge of exposing a VIP paedophile ring. She'd received death threats after joining a campaign to help children spot paedophiles. Just months before she died, she had approached BBC chiefs about her concerns with a dossier on the evidence. The friend told the *Daily Express*: 'I don't recall the names of all the stars now [well, of course not!] and I don't want to implicate anyone [of course not!] but Jill said they were surprisingly big names.' The BBC said it had seen no evidence to substantiate the claims that Jill had raised concerns over a high-profile paedophile ring.

Jill Dando's fiancé, Alan Farthing, who'd been with her the night before the killing, made no moves to push for an investigation, other than what was already taking place. He was later awarded the prestigious and lucrative appointment as Queen Elizabeth's new gynaecologist.

In a 'completely unrelated' footnote, a victim of the disgraced paedophile Bishop of Gloucester, Peter Ball, claimed that it was the bishop's friendship with Prince Charles that had made him 'impregnable'. David Greenwood, a solicitor for the survivors of Ball, spoke of how the disgraced bishop spent years cultivating relationships with those in power. 'With more power comes the ability to work in a culture where you feel that you can get away with it. It seems Peter Ball has been able to do that.'

The bishop was eventually caught and sentenced. One of his victims said of him: 'He told me how well he got on with the Queen Mother. He kept mentioning his friendship with Prince Charles in a flippant way, as anyone would talk about their friends.

One of his victims said: 'He would rub his head and say, "What can we do to really enter into the suffering of Christ, what can we do? What can you think of? Something so disgusting, so humiliating, can you think?'"

Prince Charles released a long nineteen-paragraph rebuttal of any suggestion that he'd ever sought to influence investigations into the bishop's activities, which concluded:

> ...throughout my life, my position has occasionally brought me into contact with prominent people who have subsequently been accused of serious wrong-doing. Rather than rushing to private judgement, I have always taken the view that the judicial process should take its course. I am then able to ground my opinions in facts tested by law, rather than hearsay.

In October 2015, Ball was sentenced for misconduct in public office and indecent assaults over a period of fifteen years. He died in 2019. It was a remarkable misfortune indeed then, that our monarch experienced lightning striking twice in a such an eerily-similar manner.

Charles Lynton

IN HIS EARLY YEARS AT UNIVERSITY, Tony Blair aspired to be a rock musician — he played rudimentary guitar in a band called Ugly Rumours. But it was the later 'ugly rumours' he presented to Parliament, concerning Saddam Hussein's 'weapons of mass destruction' (that never existed) for which he became better remembered.

I was fortunate that, in life, I brushed up against Tony Blair only once. At the time, I was living in a cottage in the countryside, opposite a small inn and hotel. I sometimes spent the evening chatting with the waiters and bar staff there. One evening, the place was graced by the arrival and presence of Tony Blair.

At an opportune moment, one of the staff asked for a selfie with him, and he duly obliged. In a split second, he turned on that rictus grin (not unlike the one that Richard Branson often displays). The transformation was immediate and remarkable. It brought to mind the saying, 'There's nothing more important in life than sincerity, and once you can fake that...'

Back in 1983, a man well-known to local police was charged by Bow Street Magistrates with soliciting sex with a man in a public convenience in West London, not knowing that the place was being watched by the police. The man, a promiscuous young man with long hair and girlish looks, was known in his circle as 'Miranda.'

When charged, he used his actual middle names, Charles Lynton, to disguise his identity. The man who was later to become British Prime Minister has the full name Anthony Charles Lynton Blair.

After graduating from Oxford in 1975, Tony Blair enrolled as a pupil-barrister at Lincoln's Inn. The head of his chambers, Lord Irvine, used to joke that young Blair was, 'the star that was closest to Uranus.' It was at this time that Blair also joined the Labour Party, working for the Shoreditch and Hackney South branches, until the case mentioned went before the magistrates. He'd already come to the attention of MI5 as a both a potential future minister and someone who was caught importuning young men in public toilets.

At Bow Street, Blair was fined £50 and bound over to keep the peace. The judge in his case was one, Lord Levy, who ordered a 'D Notice' to be slapped on the whole incident, meaning it couldn't be made public, 'for reasons of national security.' It probably did no harm that Miranda's elder brother, Sir William, was also a high court judge.

Lord Levy eventually became CEO of Magnet Records, before spending nine years as Blair's unelected special envoy to the Middle East. He was later the subject of a tax-avoidance scandal when it came to light that, in one particular year, he'd paid just £5000 in income tax.

Levy

It's speculated that the CIA and the FBI used the information about Blair's earlier escapades to blackmail him in to supporting the US invasion of

Iraq in 2003. Either way, his reputation as a mediocre musician makes you wonder if Adolf Hitler had been anything better than a fourth-rate painter, then he may never have ventured into politics, and millions might not have perished. Similarly, if Blair had been anything better than a fourth-rate musician, hundreds of thousands of lives in the Middle East, including those of British soldiers, might have been spared.

Tony Blair — bisexual, liar, war criminal, globalist — is believed to have amassed a fortune of somewhere between £100- and £250-million since leaving office. When nominated for a knighthood in the 2022 New Year's Honours List, a petition to have the offer rescinded reached 700,000 signatures in four days. One commentator described Blair as, 'a turd that won't be flushed.' In my own view, Blair appears to be gradually morphing into the Simpson's character, the evil Mr. Burns.

You won't find anything about the 'Charles Lynton' affair in the mainstream media. But if you search 'Charles Lynton, Bow Street' you'll find many links to sites that cover the 'alleged' incident. ...Anyway, at this point, isn't it a little redundant to try and smear Tony Blair? Is there anybody left in the world that thinks highly of him?

Justin Castreau

THE CANADIAN PRIME MINISTER, PIERRE TRUDEAU, met Margaret Sinclair when he was forty-eight and she was eighteen. When they married, five years later, he would be turning sixty, while she was only just out of her twenties. The marriage surprised Canada because Trudeau had been a lifelong playboy.

According to a 2009 *Globe and Mail* article by Margaret Wente, the *Superman* actress Margo Kidder; classical guitarist, Liona Boyd; and actresses Kim Cattrall and Barbara Streisand, had all slept with Pierre at some time. At one point he was entertaining women three at a time.

But Margaret was no saint. She smuggled drugs in the Prime Minister's official luggage, sneaked away from official functions to get out of it, and partied, scantily-clad, at Studio 54. She became embroiled in scandal for having sex with Ted Kennedy, and had the obligatory affair with a Rolling Stone — this time, Ronnie Wood.

The list went on. She was clearly attracted to men in positions of power, even those who were old and unattractive. She later attributed her wild behaviour to her bipolar disorder and self-control issues. She later went on to be a campaigner for mental-health problems.

However, the Cuban leader, Fidel Castro, put both Pierre and Margaret Trudeau to shame. His 'appetite' was legendary — he needed two fresh women every single day and would send aides out to scout for them. He fathered eleven acknowledged children but probably had many more illegitimate ones.

As Marxists, the Trudeaus adored Castro and made several trips to Cuba during the embargo era solely to see him. In April 1971, they took a long trip around the Caribbean, but visited one island they declined to mention. Although they were happy to declare all the other locations they visited, they asked the press for privacy over one 'undisclosed' island.

Eight-and-a-half months later, on Christmas Day, 1971, Justin Trudeau was born. In order for Fidel Castro to be his father, his mother would've had to be somewhere near Cuba around March/April of that year. She was.

When the Trudeaus met Castro officially for the first time, both showed an unusual amount of familiarity considering it was supposed to be their first meeting. Margaret was photographed intimately touching Fidel as he held the young Justin.

Due to Pieere's age and previous lack of children, rumour had it that Castro was the biological father of Justin. His claim that Justin was born long before the couple travelled to Cuba is based only on the official dates Pierre Trudeau visited, in his official capacity as prime minister. As Justin grew up, there wasn't a lot of room for doubt about his parentage.

As an ageing playboy, Pierre Trudeau fathered no known children, despite having been sexually promiscuous throughout his whole adult life. When he became Prime Minister, it suited him to get married and demonstrate some conventional stability. Sperm banks barely existed back then, in order to have a family, his wife had been forced to do it the old-fashioned way.

In 2000, Fidel Castro made a rare appearance outside Cuba to attend Pierre Trudeau's funeral in Canada. Later, Justin Trudeau was the only leader of the Western world to give Castro a positive eulogy without addressing his many misdeeds.

We remember Fidel Castro as an old man, but he was one of the more-impressive people in the world back then, to fellow Marxists like the Trudeaus. With his band of rag-tag rebels, Castro had forcefully deposed a brutal dictator, as he went on to turn Cuba into the West's first communist outpost. He beat away an American armed invasion while personally commanding the battle in a tank. He survived CIA coups and assassination attempts. He looked like he could beat up any other world leader. He was full of bravado, confidence, and masculine power. Why would Pierre Trudeau want anyone else to father his son?

[

Perhaps the most-credible confirmation is found in a handwritten note left by 68-year-old Fidel Castro Diaz-Balart, the eldest of Fidel Castro's 'own' children, in which he confirmed the long-running rumour that Fidel Castro 'gave birth' to Justin Trudeau after a meeting with Margaret Trudeau in 1970, and that the Canadian Prime Minister, Justin Trudeau, was indeed his half-brother.

Barry and Michael

IN JULY 2014, I was in a hotel in New York, in my room watching TV, when I realized that I was seeing was what was actually happening a couple of hundred yards down the street. On the way in to a city bookstore, where she was attending a gay wedding between two of her fans, the comedian Joan Rivers had been stopped by a reporter who asked her whether the US would ever see a gay president...

...to which Ms Rivers responded, 'What do you mean? We've already got one! Obama is gay, so let's just calm down.' She started to walk away before turning and adding, '...and Michelle is a tranny.' When the reporter asked her to explain what she'd just said, she replied, '...a transgender ...everyone knows that!' The conspiracy theories began a few weeks later when, on September 4, Joan Rivers died while undergoing what was thought to be a routine operation.

If you explore the subject further — photos, videos, and Obama's 'mis-speaking' — it makes you begin to wonder. As ever, 'factcheckers' will refute it all, or contrive plausible explanations, but can you simply discount it all as misinformation or mischief making?

During the eight years of Obama's official presidency (not counting the years he has spent pulling the strings of the Biden puppet) more than once, Barak Obama referred to 'Michael' and not Michelle. In one speech, Obama corrects himself after stating, 'Michael and I....'

Dr Rafael Espinanzo, who was entrusted with former First Lady Michelle Obama's care during the 2008 presidential election, spoke out, feeling that the public needed a genuine eyewitness:

> Michelle Obama is not a woman who used to be a man. Michelle Obama is just a man —with breast implants and a huge shaving bill. On the campaign trail, no medical staff were allowed to go near her other than to take her medicine if she got sick, which she never did. I walked into a room where she was taking a leak — and I was paid millions to remain silent.

An Obama spokesman responded: 'Whatever information the doctor has is privileged. Should he decide to trade his license and every dime he's ever made for a few minutes of fame, so be it.' But there has never been any direct rebuttal of Dr Espinanzo's accusations, nor any attempt at legal redress.

There are videos, not hidden, that clearly show Michelle making some kind of adjustment to her groin area, and photographs that reveal some kind of bulge there. Of course, with AI and photoshop some, or many of these, including images of her birth certificate as a male might be explained as mischief or fakes. But again, it's happened often enough to make you wonder.

There are the photos of the Michelle looking distinctly masculine that may or may not be doctored. But some unaltered images reveal someone with a strong jaw, wide shoulders, and large hands — and looking, if anything, a lot sturdier and more-robust than her husband.

People cite the Obamas' two children, which Michelle says were conceived via IVF. But many have pointed out how much their daughters, Sasha and Malia, look like a couple that have long been closely associated with the Obamas. Anita Blanchard is the OB/gyn who 'delivered' both girls; while her partner Marty Nesbitt worked as Barak's campaign treasurer. The Nesbitts and the Obamas are not only close associates and neighbours but attend sports matches and go on vacation together. You can see the reason for the debate...

But aside from all the speculation, what is maybe more concerning is Barak Obama's somewhat sketchy background... American Ann Dunham met Kenyan Muslim, Barrack Obama (Senior) in Hawaii, where they were studying Russian. They married six months before they welcomed their son, in 1961. The boy was named after his father and his birthplace registered as Hawaii. Ann Dunham later remarried a man called Lolo Soetoro and her new husband legally adopted the boy, who was registered as 'Barry Soetoro' (and as a Muslim) in Jakarta.

The idea that America's 44th President was really born outside the United States, and the details later amended, has always been a hot topic. And there is evidence that 'Barry' was not actually born on American soil, later covered up, as it would've made him ineligible to be an American president.

Big Issue | Financial Standard | Maddo | Pulse | Style | Society
Sunday, June 27, 2004

Kenyan-born Obama all set for US Senate

Kenyan-born US Senate hopeful, Barrack Obama, appeared set to take over the Illinois Senate seat after his main rival, Jack Ryan, dropped out of the race on Friday night amid a furor over lurid sex club allegations.

The allegations that horrified fellow Republicans and caused his once-promising candidacy to implode in four short days have given Obama a clear lead as Republicans struggled to fetch an alternative.

Ryan's campaign began to crumble on Monday following the release of embarrassing records from his divorce. In the records, his ex-wife, Boston Public actress Jeri Ryan, said her former husband took her to club

Barrack Obama

Even though there are early newspaper articles about Obama that describe him as Kenyan. It's said that the Supreme Court 'overlooked' this matter as they feared that ruling Obama ineligible for office would have triggered race riots and maybe even civil war.

There are also reports about Barry Soetoro's time as a prominent figure on the Chicago gay scene, where his leisure activities earned him the nickname 'Bathhouse Barry' But, it's not illegal to be gay. What is more worrying is Barry's entire political trajectory.

When he was 10-years-old, Barry was sent to live in Hawaii. with his grandparents, who were communists. He soon met their close friend, Frank Marshall Davis, another well-known communist and Labour Union activist with whom he developed a strong bond. Barry considered him as a mentor and was greatly influenced by him. 'I chose my friends carefully,' he later wrote '...politically-active black students ...Marxist professors, and feminists...'

Whilst in college Obama met wealthy Muslims. One of these was his roommate, Mohammad Hassan Chandoo, with whom he made a trip to Pakistan.

Obama was fascinated by his friend's lifestyle and it's alluded to that they had a gay relationship, but his 2008 election campaign made sure this rumour was well-hidden from the media, until Obama accidentally mentioned their trip. Chandoo later became a major campaigner for Obama and raised $100,000 for him. Obama went on to attend Harvard, left with a law degree, and moved to Chicago to become an attorney — where he had to swear an oath that he'd never been known legally by any other name.

He was inspired by a book called *Rules for Radicals,* by the neo-Marxist, Saul Alinsky. who claimed that 'community organizers' should be, among other things, narcissistic, amoral, and able to promote things they didn't believe in — in other words, good at lying.

Alinsky detailed the eight factors that must be controlled in order to create a 'social' state, the first of which is the most important: 1) Healthcare 2) Poverty 3) Debt 4) Gun Control 5) Welfare 6) Education 7) Religion 8) Class Warfare.

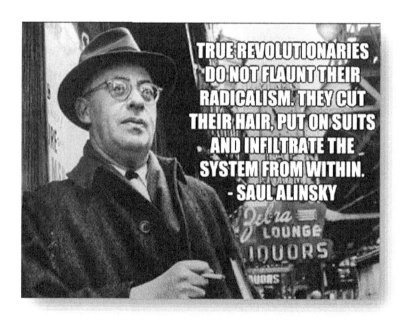

There's little doubt that Alinsky's idea of a better system simply means a communist regime. But his methods and philosophy have had a profound influence right across one side of the political divide in the United States. Recent history suggests that this influence has been nothing short of catastrophic.

During his presidential campaign, Obama's work as a 'community organizer' was portrayed as something for the public to admire — as it supposedly demonstrated his connection to the people — through his work for the Association of Community Organizations for Reform. Sadly, ACORN was later found to have embezzled around $5 million and was investigated in over fourteen different states for voter fraud. Obama represented them as lawyer.

Obama also represented a Lebanese developer, Tony Rezko, who was convicted of corruption charges and given a ten-year sentence, and who was alleged to have raised more than $14m for Obama's U.S. Senate campaign. Though, inevitably, he was also heavily funded by George Soros.

Who else helped get Obama into the White House? There's no journalistic interest in the regular media to go digging, as it certainly wouldn't serve the interests of their shared owners.

At the time of writing, Obama's personal chef, Tafari Campbell, died in an unlikely accident in which he, as an accomplished surfer, fell from his surfboard and drowned in the water fronting the Obama property. The mainstream fact-checkers were already denying that the chef was about to go public with new revelations, even before any accusations had actually been made!

* * *

Honestly, where do we start... where do we finish? After all, we haven't even touched on Harry and Meghan yet!! For instance, what about Meghan's disaster with the 'moon bump' – when her 'pregnancy' dislodged and slipped down between her knees?

Did she actually give birth? Did they use a surrogate? Could Meghan Markle have even given birth — given that she may be good few years older than claimed? ...Given that her old classmates from college are all somehow five years older than she is. And has anyone ever seen the kids – Archie and Lilibet – apart from a couple of vague photos, or were they also borrowed?

All of this is mere trivia and gossip once you start looking into the plane loads of gold being flown around the world, or into Rupert and Ghislaine Maxwell's connections to the Israeli secret service, Mossad — or the enigmatic death of Castrudeau's brother, Michel, due to a 'freak accident.' ...And don't even mention the Epstein Island flight logs, 9/11, the assassination of JFK, fake alien invasion, or the moon landing, rigged elections, the Antarctica 'no-fly' zone, or the strange murals at Denver airport... Strange affairs indeed... where do we start...?

So, let's finish off, for now, with one of the more-unpleasant characters to have slid down the pipe in recent times...

Klaus Schwab

'Vell com, Meester Bond,
vee haff bien expectink you....'

YOU CAN ALMOST HEAR THE WORDS spilling from the slobbering jowls of Klaus Schwab — a third-rate James Bond villain if ever there was one. But one that even Central Casting might reject as being too obvious. But Schwab 'the man' is anything but a joke. He is a dangerous, decadent, and intent on controlling every aspect of your life and mine. If you're not yet aware of Klaus Schwab and his lifelong project known as the World Economic Forum, then I suggest you read on...

Simply stated, Schwab wants what he calls a 'global reset' — which amounts to a new feudal system using technology to round up and control the rest of us serfs into compliance with his agenda — which he believes will happen because he's just 'so fucking Schmart'. His proudest boast is how he has infiltrated all the governments of the Western world.

...Here he is cavorting, in matching floral shirt, with (the equally-unelected) British prime minister, Rishi Sunak, and (the equally-unpopular) Justin Castrudeau.

Even if you've never heard of Klaus Schwab, you'll have heard his catchphrases, like 'Build Back Better,' parroted around the world. Another favourite is '...you vill own nus-sink, unt you vill be heppy.' And if that makes him sound like a caricature of a Nazi villain, then it's not without good reason — his father was one of Hitler's generals.

Since history began, many an Egyptian pharaoh, Asian warlord, Roman emperor, Tsar, King, and Fuhrer has sought the conquest of nations and absolute power over the rest of humanity. One empire after another: Assyrian, Babylonian, Chinese, Persian, Roman, Spanish, British, and American.

This lust is just as alive and dangerous today as it has ever been.

In the past, invading other nations involved boots on the ground, steel against steel, and every blast answered with a bigger blast. Today, there's no need for swords and spears, machine guns or missiles. The new 'invaders' simply create a terrible danger that threatens us all, knowing that most people will immediately surrender all their rights and freedoms in order to be made 'safe'.

China is often touted by globalists like Castrudeau as the ideal model for the New World Order — an entire country covered by constant surveillance through digital ID and facial recognition. Those that fail to comply with this system are not able to ride trains, access bank accounts, buy food, or find employment. In the West, other method are being used — via the onslaught of 'wokeness' and 'cancel culture' — the prohibition of free speech, methods of censorship, deletion of bank accounts, state-controlled journalism, and psychological warfare.

Of course, many don't see any of this. 'Ha ha! that's conspiracy theory!' they chorus. It's such a potent display of stupidity, yet it's the perception of many. Try to explain that powerful people with unlimited financial resources are already dominating the world, and you'll be met with a blank stare.

Schwab's World Economic Forum — the beast he's devoted his entire life to nurturing — works hand in glove with presidents, bankers, and the CEOs of the world's largest corporations. It glues together the self-interests of billionaires and trillionaires like Bill Gates, George Soros, the Rockefellers, and the Rothschilds (...Schwab's own mother was Marianne Rothschild).

Their vast financial resources have put in place political stooges, through election fraud, if necessary, to determine the direction of healthcare, business, finance, and all the rest of it, around the world. The World Economic Forum is the Big Brother of all humanity — although no-one has ever elected any of its members or given consent. The voice of humanity doesn't count.

The WEF cloaks itself in bland policies like 'improving the state of the world' or 'global goals for sustainable development'. But the intention is full control over business, health, and information, etc. The WEF also claims the noble goal of 'ending poverty.' But the only way this could be done is by us all having to take weekly benefit handout that has to be earned by total compliance.

The true objective becomes clear when we look at how they plan to end poverty so that every person on is dependent on these overlords. 'Imagine no possessions,' sang John Lennon. Now imagine also having no voice, no privacy, and no freedom.

The global reset also involves the creation of 'smart cities' — hi-tech urban areas with micro-chipped citizens, where every aspect of our lives is monitored — every conversation, every purchase, all physical activity, and location.

Klaus Schwab's assistant psychopath, the creepy Yuval Noah Harari, has openly stated that, 'free will is a thing of the past,' and 'humans are hackable animals' as he savours the prospect of chipping people to control our emotions and even our very DNA.

Participation in society — access to banking services, shopping, gatherings, social activities, transport, health care, and so on, will depend on your vaccination status, or your carbon credit, or some other bogus qualification connected to a digital ID and social acceptability score.

Yuval Noah Harari

Another WEF goal is 'zero hunger'. While that again sounds admirable, in reality, it means eating insects and lab grown 'meat.' Bill Gates works closely with the WEF, buying up all the farmland in America, while setting up factories where synthetic meat is produced. By some strange quirk of fate, in the past few years, more than a hundred of America's largest food production and distribution plants have suffered fires and burned to the ground. In 2022, more than fifteen of the leading food companies had their headquarters go up in flames — in the same week! ...Nothing to see here, folks.

In the Netherlands, the government orders farmers to kill much of their livestock, as traditional farming is strategically eliminated, so that the population becomes totally dependent on the 'food' provided by the financial elites. In Australia, growing your own food is being outlawed, for 'biosecurity' reasons. While in the UK, the government claims that gardening is one of the causes of heart disease! Make no mistake, 'zero hunger' is all about discouraging and eventually forbidding people to grow their own food, in order to make the entire world dependent on the shit provided by the rulers.

Now, the upside to all this indescribable madness, is that it's all being pushed way too far, too fast, too soon. The original plan was to introduce all of this stuff gradually by 2030, or even 2050. But with people already beginning to wake up and resist, the powers have to try and ram everything through all at once. But unfortunately for Anal Schwab, his Great Reset is turning into a Great Awakening as more and more people begin to understand what is going on in our world.

Schwab probably likes to think of himself as some kind of glorious emperor.

By contrast, this image is an actual picture of him on the beach, and looking a less than inspiring. It's not difficult for even the most-amateur psychologist to see where his overweening ambition, vanity, and lust for power comes from. Hitler famously had only one testicle. Along with his drooping man-boobs and skinny chicken legs, Klaus Schwab's ambitions are a great example of a man with 'two-inch dick' syndrome.

For centuries, we've moaned about our governments, but have been clueless about the powers that really rule from behind the scenes. But now there is hope for the future. Now, at last, we are starting to see who the real villains are, and how insanely evil is their agenda. It is now time for the greatest mass awakening in all history. It's time to bind the enemies of humanity and release the world from their vile grip.

THE END.

If you enjoyed this book (and even if you didn't)
you may enjoy some of the author's other work...

Rough Notes

Rough Notes takes the reader through Bruce's earliest days, from learning to play the bass, to his meteoric rise as a sought-after player. His experiences and run-ins with some of music's greatest legends are detailed throughout. Bruce is a walking history of rock and roll, which makes this memoir one of the most-important ever written. It's an unflinching account of the life of the working musician, and tells the reader about the rise of Elvis Costello and the Attractions, one of the great bands in rock and roll history, from a matter-of-fact, front-row seat point-of-view. But none of it takes away from the whirlwind ride that is *Rough Notes*. I am normally a slow reader, but I got through all 493 pages in 3 days.

The Open Road

*Amazon ***** reviews*

This book gathers thoughts, some (but not all) woven around the experiences of travelling, written in Bruce Thomas' very engaging style. You have the occasional music reference, of course, but that's not central to the book. Central to the book is his mind, gently purring away.

Always interesting, never afraid to be controversial or unconventional, challenging, full of insights into life's journey, a man who's travelled many roads, from the very heights of fame, to personal struggles; a man with things to relate to you that shouldn't be ignored. Highly recommended to anyone sharp and savvy enough to take on the questions.

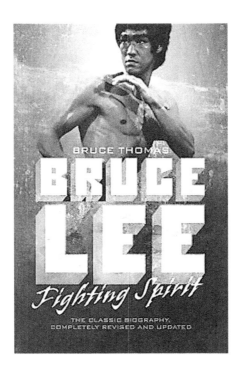

Fighting Spirit

'An endlessly stimulating account of Lee's life and times.'
Loaded

'Deserves to find acclaim far beyond
the circles of martial arts enthusiasts.' *FHM*

'A belting read ...as hard-hitting as the Little Dragon's fabled
one-inch punch.' *Maxim Book of the Month*

Bruce Thomas has gone to extreme lengths to make this book a good read. He has succeeded. This book is a masterpiece in its own right, not just because of the subject matter, but because of the way the story of an important person has been told.

A book that's worth every penny, whether you're interested in martial arts or not. There is still only one REAL biography of Bruce Lee. And *this* is it.

This is probably the clearest, sanest account of the man's life you'll get. Also has the best suggestion I've heard about how he died.

A Life Worth Remembering: 50th Anniversary Edition
...is a condensed version of the text of *Fighting Spirit*, updated with new interviews and recently-revealed information. A large-format, full-colour book with over 400 images, many of them rare. This is the book that sold out within the first hour of its release.

Printed in Great Britain
by Amazon

37658067R00088